The West Wind

A Winnipesaukee Sailing Adventure

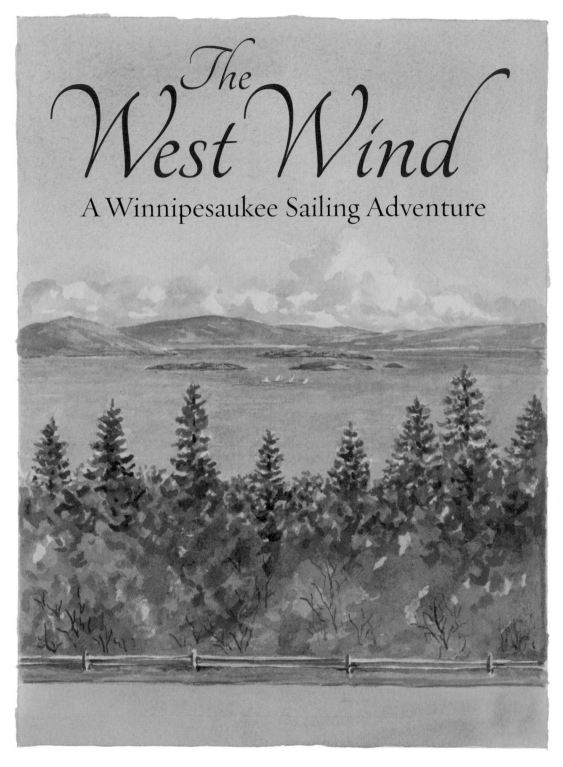

by Andy Opel

Illustrated by Karel Hayes and John Gorey

Jetty House
Portsmouth, NH
2023

Dedicated to the founders, board, and staff of the Lake
Winnipesaukee Sailing Association – AO

To all of our family and friends who are sailors – JG & KH

The Lake Winnipesaukee Sailing Association is located in Gilford,
New Hampshire, on Smith Cove. The association was founded to promote
and expand participation in the sport of sailing, particularly on Lake
Winnipesaukee. Our goals are to remove barriers of knowledge, financial
means, disability, and age. LWSA is a non-profit charity for the benefit of the
people and communities of the Lakes Region now and for generations to come.
In carrying out our mission, we pledge to foster safety, self-confidence, teamwork,
honesty, positive sporting values, and an appreciation for our environment.
To learn more about the LWSA, visit our website https://www.lwsa.org/.

LAKE WINNIPESAUKEE
SAILING ASSOCIATION

info@lwsa.org   www.lwsa.org

© 2023 Andy Opel
Illustrations © 2023 by Karel Hayes and John Gorey

ISBN: 978-1-937721-98-5
Library of Congress Control Number: 2023904818

Printed in China

Published by
Jetty House
an imprint of Peter E. Randall Publisher LLC
5 Greenleaf Woods Drive, Suite 102
Portsmouth, NH 03801
www.perpublisher.com

lakewinniadventures.com

Every summer, Jack, Franny, and J.J. counted down the last days of school because they were so excited to go see Grammy at the lake.

Early June was cool and the lake was still chilly for swimming, but that didn't stop the kids from running off the dock and racing out to the raft. They always went swimming the first day they arrived—no matter how cold it was!

"Now that you are here, the summer can begin!" said Grammy.

"I have a surprise for you," she said, showing the kids a brochure. "I made arrangements for all three of you to go to the sailing school in Smith Cove. Classes start next week!"

"You mean we have to go back to school?" asked Franny.

"But we just finished school, Grammy," protested Jack. "We don't go to school in the summer."

"Will I have to take a sailing test?" asked J.J. "I don't like tests."

"Well, this is not like any school you have ever been to," said Grammy. "Here they'll teach you valuable skills that you need to know if you are going to live on the lake. You never know when you might need sailing skills," she added.

The following week, Grammy took the children over to the first day of sailing school.

"Hi, Franny, Jack, and J.J! I'm Ben. Welcome to the sailing school. Franny and Jack, you'll be working with me. J.J., you are in Cat's Mighty Mini class."

"I'm scared Grammy," said J.J., looking at the other kids and wondering if he could really sail a boat all by himself.

"It's OK to be nervous J.J., but you need to remember that these teachers are very good at their jobs and will keep you safe while they teach you to sail," said Grammy.

"Come on J.J., we are going to start with some games," said Cat as she took J.J. by the hand and introduced him to the other students.

"Wow, I almost capsized," cried J.J., when a gust of wind caught his sail.

He waved to Franny and Jack, who were sailing a larger boat.

"Let's tack upwind," said Franny,
moving the tiller as Jack pulled
in the mainsheet.

"This is amazing," cried Jack.

At the top of the bay, they came about
and headed for the dock on a broad reach.

SAIL
MAIN SHEET
SPREADERS
SHROUDS
FORESTAY
MAST.....

WIND

COME
ABOUT

JIBING

By the end of the day, all the kids knew a lot of new names for the parts of the sailboat.

"How was your first day of sailing school?" asked Grammy when the kids returned to the house.

"I liked sailing the Opti," said J.J.

"Jack and I sailed a 420," added Franny. "I was the skipper."

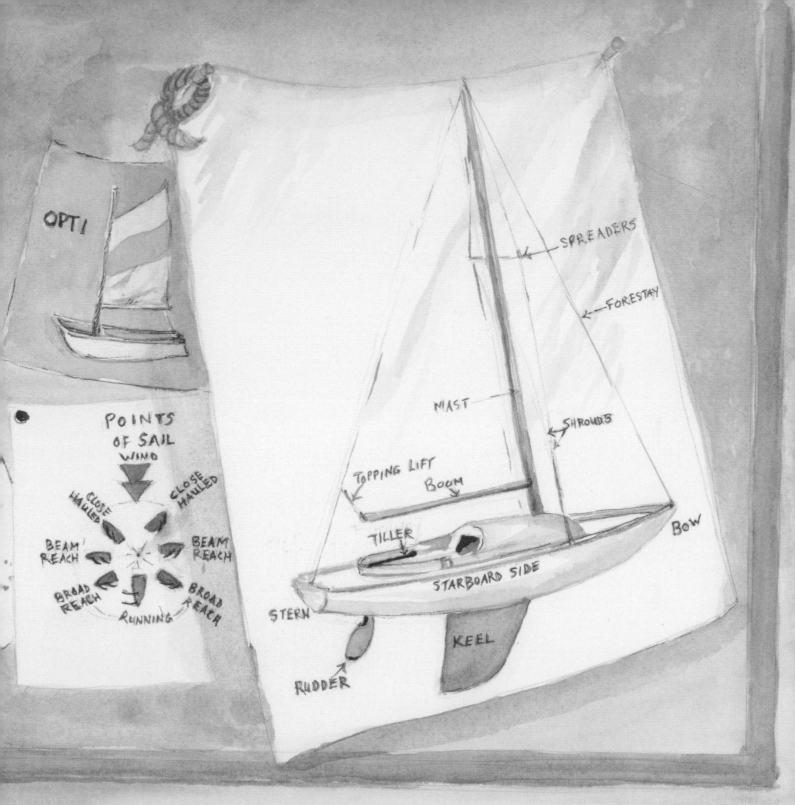

"There sure are a lot of funny words in sailing," noted J.J. "I don't know why there are sheets and booms and jibs. I get confused sometimes when they tell me to jibe."

"We were close-hauled when we tacked upwind," said Jack. "We were going really fast and both of us had to sit on the edge of the boat to keep it from capsizing."

"Wow, I am so impressed," said Grammy. "You are learning all the proper terms, and more importantly, you are learning how to sail!"

The next day, as they were getting in the car to go to sailing school, Mr. Fuller stopped by to say hello.

"Welcome back to the lake! Where are you all going?" he asked.

"We're going to sailing school," replied Jack.

"Sailing school?" asked Mr. Fuller, looking skeptical. "Why would you do that? You have a motorboat . . . and now you know where The Witches are so you don't have to worry about hitting those rocks."

"Sailing is really fun," said Franny. "You don't need a motor and the wind pushes the boat really fast."

"But the wind doesn't always blow," replied Mr. Fuller. "Engines are more reliable, but have fun at sailing school," he added, waving to the kids as they drove away.

On the last day of sailing school, all the students sailed
in a couple of larger boats and went to a protected cove
on Fish Island. They anchored the boats, and everyone ate
lunch, swam and played on the rocks around the shore.

When Grammy picked them up at the end of the two-week class, the teachers came out to give her a report about what the kids had learned.

"J.J. was a great student. He's graduated to the next level," said Cat.

"Thank you, Cat!" said J.J. "You really helped me when I was scared."

"And Jack and Franny were an incredible team," added Ben. "They really shared the work and took turns being skipper. I would love to see them come back and join our racing club."

"That sounds amazing," said Jack, excited by the idea of racing.

"Thank you for a great class, Ben," said Franny. "I really learned a lot. Racing sounds like fun. See you next year!"

On the ride home, the three sailors were sad to finish sailing school but when they got back to Boulder Lodge, Grammy had a surprise for them.

"I bought this old sailboat that needs a little work. When you come back in the fall, the boat will be ready," said Grammy. "In the fall, the water is still warm and the wind will be great for sailing."

When Jack, Franny, and J.J. returned in late September for a long weekend, the leaves were turning golden yellow, the air was clear and cool, and the wind was blowing hard, just like Grammy had predicted.

"That is a west wind and those white caps tell us the wind is blowing over ten miles an hour," Grammy said, pointing out at the blustery lake. "You'll need to use all your sailing skills to keep the boat from capsizing."

"We can do it!" exclaimed Jack, as they began to rig the sails.

Franny took the tiller, Jack grabbed the mainsheet, and J.J. held the jib sheet. They all had to sit on the windward side of the boat as the wind filled the sails and made the boat heel over. They tacked upwind, back and forth across Saunders Bay, laughing as they sailed through the choppy water, the wind and waves bouncing and splashing the boat.

"Watch out Franny, that is a buoy for The Witches," warned Jack.

"Oh no, not The Witches again," said J.J. nervously.

"OK, we need to tack NOW ," declared Franny, giving the command and pushing the tiller away from her. They climbed under the boom as it moved across the boat, Jack pulling the mainsheet and J.J. making the jib come around to the other side of the mast.

As they got closer to Governor's Island, Jack noticed a boat bobbing in the waves.

"That's Mr. Fuller," said Jack. "It looks like he's in trouble."

The kids sailed toward Mr. Fuller's boat. As they got close, Jack let the mainsail out so the boat slowed down.

"I ran out of gas," said Mr. Fuller. "Do you think you could go to my boathouse and bring me the gas can? I put my anchor down, so I'll wait here."

"Sure!" yelled Jack, excited by the challenge of helping to rescue Mr. Fuller.

Franny steered the boat downwind, and they headed toward
Mr. Fuller's boathouse.

Franny and J.J. held the sailboat at the dock while Jack got the
gas can out of the boathouse and brought it back to the sailboat.

Tacking back and forth upwind, the kids made it back to
Mr. Fuller without spilling any gas. As they approached Mr. Fuller's
boat, Franny put the sailboat into irons, pointing directly into the
wind, and they slipped right alongside Mr. Fuller's boat.

"Nice driving, Franny," Mr. Fuller said as Jack handed him the gas can. "You really saved me. There are not many boats out this time of year." Mr. Fuller poured the gas into his boat's tank, started the engine, and pulled up his anchor. The kids had already sailed downwind and were headed straight for Grammy's dock.

As they were de-rigging the boat, Mr. Fuller pulled up to the dock.

"You sure have some skilled grandchildren," Mr. Fuller said to Grammy.
"*They* rescued *me* this time!" he added with a big smile on his face.

"Well, you know what they taught us in sailing school?" Jack asked. "Real boaters don't need motors!" All the kids laughed and Mr. Fuller nodded his head in agreement.

THE END